C000298905

RAILS ACROSS EUROPE

EASTERN AND SOUTHERN EUROPE

RAILS ACROSS EUROPE

EASTERN AND SOUTHERN EUROPE

DAVID CABLE

First published in Great Britain in 2016 by
Pen & Sword Transport
An imprint of Pen & Sword Books Ltd
47 Church Street
Barnsley
South Yorkshire
S70 2AS

ISBN 978 1 47384 432 2

Printed and bound in India by Replika Press Pvt. Ltd.

Pen & Sword Books Ltd incorporates the imprints of Pen & Sword Archaeology, Atlas, Aviation, Battleground, Discovery, Family History, History, Maritime, Military, Naval, Politics, Railways, Select, Social History, Transport, True Crime, and Claymore Press, Frontline Books, Leo Cooper, Praetorian Press, Remember When, Seaforth Publishing and Wharncliffe.

For a complete list of Pen & Sword titles please contact
Pen & Sword Books Limited
47 Church Street, Barnsley, South Yorkshire, S70 2AS, England
E-mail: enquiries@pen-and-sword.co.uk
Website: www.pen-and-sword.co.uk

DAVID CABLE – OTHER PUBLICATIONS

Railfreight in Colour (for the modeller and historian)
BR Passenger Sectors in Colour (for the modeller and historian)
Lost Liveries of Privatisation in Colour (for the modeller and historian)
Hydraulics in the West
The Blue Diesel Era
Rails Across North America – A Pictorial Journey across the USA
Rails Across Canada – A Pictorial Journey across Canada
Rails Across Europe – Northern and Western

Introduction

During the nineteenth century, railways developed throughout the Mediterranean, Central European and Balkan countries, in most cases with state involvement, although Switzerland had more privately financed lines than most other countries. Lines were, in the main, of standard gauge as originally established in Great Britain, namely 4' 8½" (1435mm), with the major exceptions of the Ukraine, which as part of the original Romanov empire used 5' 0" (1520mm), whilst the Iberian peninsula countries – Spain and Portugal – adopted 5' 6" (1668mm). And especially in Switzerland and to a lesser extent Austria, a large number of narrow metre gauge lines were built, some of which are quite extensive, providing, for example, a through service from St Moritz to Zermatt. The difference in gauges has created problems on the main lines in the past, necessitating the transhipment of loads from one wagon to another, but improvements in bogie design have started to overcome this aspect.

Generally the systems remained as originally built, until the 1930s, when the Italians built the Direttissima High Speed line from Bologna to Firenze so as to avoid a route with severe operating restrictions due to the topography in that area. Then in the early 1980s, the first of a new generation of High Speed lines opened with the building of the LGV line from Paris to Lyon in France, which has subsequently fostered extensions through to Marseille and Montpellier, further lines to reach the Tours and Strasbourg areas, with plans to develop an LGV through to Bordeaux. In Italy, new High Speed lines now link Milano and Roma, with several other lines at the planning stage, whilst Spain now connects Barcelona, Madrid and Seville with the AVE network, which is being further extended to encompass Valencia amongst other cities. Several other countries are also considering the provision of specific lines on this model as an alternative to improving existing tracks to reduce journey times. A classic example of this applies in Switzerland, with the opening of new tunnels through the Alps replacing the old curving routes either side of the Gotthard and Lotschberg tunnels.

One application to assist trains surmount stiff gradients has been the use of rack systems, which have enabled extremely steep lines to be built, particularly on the narrow gauge lines in Switzerland, with the maximum being an incredible 48 per cent on the Pilatus railway, and which, from personal experience, really feels it!

In comparison with Northern Europe, much of the south and east of Europe is quite mountainous, and as a result lines and motive power had to deal with a much more complex set of circumstances. Experiments in electrification were soon put into practice, especially in Switzerland and Austria, where hydro-electric power generation was available and relatively cheap. Over the years, as steam was replaced, electrified lines became widespread apart from some of the lines serving more remote areas, where costs were not justified. In general terms main lines in Southern France use 1,500 volts DC, Spain, Italy and Slovenia 3,000 volts DC, Switzerland and Austria 15kV AC and all other countries 25kV AC. Passenger services now increasingly comprise of trains using multiple electric units for both High Speed and conventional long distance and local services. As with those trains in Northern Europe, restaurant facilities are still available on some long distance services, but sleeping cars are now rare.

Freight services are all locomotive hauled, and an increasing number are intermodal or bulk carrying trains. Many services work through internationally, requiring developments in motive power to be capable of working through as much as possible to minimise delays in having to change locomotives to suit each country's particular circumstances. Open Access operators have become more prevalent in recent times, 'cherry picking' some of the more profitable business and leaving the major rail companies with the often loss-making residue. It is also noteworthy that the German company DB Schenker has developed operations into several Baltic countries.

Locomotives used in Southern Europe are, in the main, built by indigenous manufacturers such as Skoda in the Czech Republic and Ansaldo Breda in Italy. Bombardier and Siemens locomotives are widely used on through workings, and Alstom and Vossloh types can also be seen. Rather curiously, the original Eurosprinter design of Siemens was only adopted in Spain (class 252) and Portugal (class 5600), although it has been developed into the ES series.

The Open Access operators usually lease locomotives from organisations such as Dispolok, MRCE, Railpool and ELL. Of particular note is the importation to Hungary, Romania and Bulgaria of British locomotives, the class 56 and 86 diesel and electric locos used by Floyd in Hungary, and the class 87s and 92s used in the other two countries, some still carrying their British colours and names!

Other rolling stock has developed, being generally of larger capacity, all being mounted on bogies. Passenger facilities include better toilet provisions, and some limited arrangements for disabled persons compared with those in Northern Europe. Unfortunately, many southern countries suffer from epidemics of graffiti being applied to coaches and wagons, which hardly encourages passengers to use trains.

This volume has been designed to represent a selection of trains in most of the countries in the south and east of Europe, with the exception of some Balkan countries, which have not been visited by myself or friends. Some visits also took place some years ago. The pictures cover the last thirty years or so, with one or two before that. The majority of the photos are of my own taking, mostly on holidays. Some pictures were taken by Steve Sachs (now deceased), whose pictures were devoid of details, but research by Keith Fender, Brian Garvin and Nick Fotis has filled in some details. There are a few shots taken by my friends, Brian Denton, and a special selection of superb photos by Murray Lewis. My thanks to all of these people. Details of particular trains, especially freight workings, have not been available as compared with what is published in the UK, but generally passenger services have been identified.

This book is one of a pair covering the whole of Europe, so complete the pictures by reading the volume *Rails Across Europe – Northern and Western.*

David Cable
Hartley Wintney, Hants, UK
April, 2015

Notes on railways of each country

Austria
The OBB is the main state railway with substantial through workings to its neighbouring countries, and vice versa, especially Germany. Some passenger services are franchised to open access operators, as well as freight trains. The Railnet services connect Wien with the Hungarian, Slovak and Bohemian capitals with regular daily trains. There are a number of narrow gauge railways in the country, mainly providing for tourists.

Bulgaria
The BDZ state owned system comprises a mixture of standard and narrow gauge lines. Some private operators' work trains within the country, and DB Schenker has established a foothold. Electric and diesel locomotives are all of twentieth-century build dates, but some new multiple units have been introduced fairly recently.

Croatia
The Croatian Railways (HZ) was sectorised in recent times, splitting infrastructure from train operations. Rolling stock from the last century was mainly inherited from the old Yugoslav network, comprising Swedish based electric designs of locos as well as some Italian types. Diesel locos are fitted with GM engines. New multiple units have now been commissioned.

Czech Republic
The Czech railways have been a joy for the enthusiast for many years, since most trains are still locomotive hauled. Until recently there has been a bewildering variety of colour schemes, although new corporate passenger and freight schemes are now becoming more widespread. Czech trains are closely allied to those of Slovakia, with Skoda having built almost all locomotives used on both systems. Trains run through to Austria, Germany and spasmodically to Poland, as well, of course, to Slovakia. In principle, Bohemia works off 3,000 volts DC, whilst Moravia and Slovakia are on 25kV, requiring the use of many dual voltage locos. Pendolino trains were introduced for some main line services, but have not proved popular enough to be expanded, so that Railjet trains have now come to the fore. Private freight operators are seen in the country, with Metrans working widely into Germany.

France (South)
South of a line from Strasbourg to Nantes, the SNCF has expanded its TGV services through to the Mediterranean at the expense of conventional passenger trains. A reasonable amount of freight is handled, but private operators are largely restricted due to Trade Union pressures. In the remoter parts of the country, train services are, at best, poor if not downright appalling, with train schedules not helpful to potential

passengers, resulting in many services being withdrawn. Photos of trains in Northern France are included in the companion volume *Rails Across Europe – Northern and Western*.

Greece

Although some modern locomotives have been purchased in recent years, and there are some modern multiple units, much of the rolling stock is quite old. However, the financial situation in Greece has led to major cutbacks, leaving only a skeleton main line hub.

Hungary

In addition to the main MAV state railways, there are a number of other operators in Hungary, notably Gysev, jointly owned with Austria, and several private freight operators. International passenger services connect with Austria and Romania, with more local services into Slovakia. A mixture of modern and old rolling stock can be seen, ranging from Bombardier TRAXX electric locos, to Nohab diesels. The railways are generally well run, with frequent services within the country.

Italy

FS, the state Italian system, has invested in more High Speed services in recent times, whilst still running many conventional express passenger services. More and more freight trains are being worked by private operators, connecting widely with other countries through Austria and France. FS rolling stock is almost all built in Italy, whereas private operators use other standard designs.

Portugal

National financial problems have restricted development of the CP network in recent years, although Pendolino sets were built for services between Lisbon and Porto, with some extended to the Algarve area. Otherwise trains are loco hauled primarily with electric traction, which has now replaced the previous diesel worked trains south from Lisbon. Through working to Spain is sparse, with some limited private freight operations.

Romania

The CFR is the main state railway, but there are a large number of separate companies working over the network, including DB Schenker. The majority of the main lines are electrified, and there is a small element of narrow gauge lines. Locos are generally of Romanian manufacture, in the main of many years vintage.

Serbia

Serbian railways are in a very run down, unreliable state, with old rolling stock of often fifty years of age.

Slovakia

Using Czech designs exclusively for rolling stock, ZSSK trains run a mixture of long distance expresses and more localised country services, in addition to some freight operations. Private operators are very few.

Slovenia

The railways in this country have to cope with some quite mountainous terrain, and consequently have invested in some fairly high powered locomotives, in particular the Siemens Taurus, and previously the French CC6500. Both these classes work passenger and freight trains, supported by more moderate engines in the flatter parts of the country. Modern EMUs work local services, and Italian built Pendolinos run services between Ljubljana and Maribor. There are still a few locomotives inherited from the Yugoslav break up, mainly GM diesel engine units.

Spain

The Spanish have invested in standard gauge High Speed links between major cities, which system is being expanded in spite of the financial condition of the country. The rest of the network (broad gauge) is operated, generally, by modern electric and diesel locomotives, passenger trains being formed of Talgo stock. Modern EMUs work Cercanias services around Madrid and Barcelona. Most freight trains are run by the national company RENFE, although there are some private operators.

Switzerland

Swiss railways are noted for their punctuality. The standard gauge lines – SBB, BLS and SOB – all use modern electric locomotives and coaching stock, also including EMUs for local work and some tilting sets for longer distance runs. The country's mountains impose restrictions on certain routes, which investment is tending to overcome. Freight trains work international services, with Swiss cargo locos, in particular, being seen outside the Swiss borders.

The country is noted for its many narrow gauge lines and rack railways, almost all of which are privately operated by electric railcars, apart from the longer distance routes (RhB, MGB, MOB) which use high powered electric locomotives.

Turkey (in Europe)

The small part of the Turkish railways in Europe have connections with Greece and Bulgaria, but through traffic is very infrequent. There are some suburban services in Istanbul, but with the new tunnel now open under the Bosphorus, perhaps more through traffic will eventuate.

Ukraine

This country uses much rolling stock developed in Russia, from when the two countries were united. Many interesting designs in a plethora of colours can be seen on this broad gauge system, some of which are of modern construction.

Austria

The Wilder Kaiser Mountains form a backdrop to a westbound freight train passing through Kitzbuhel station, headed by OBB 1110 001-3 in May 1987.

A nice selection of light engines are seen heading east at Schwarzsee, near Kitzbuhel, in May 1987. Nearest the camera is 1020 015-2, with a class 1010 and class 1044 in the lead.

1063 021-8 attaches a van to a Bischofshofen to Worgl train at Schwarzach St Veit, in June 1992, as another train arrives on the adjacent track.

At the old station at St Anton, the VSOE bound for Venezia stops to allow passengers to stretch their legs, but why can't they learn to keep out of the way of the photographer?!! The train is hauled by 1110 519-4 in a special livery and has been banked up through the Arlberg tunnel by 1020 037-6.

With a colourful selection of vans, a westbound parcels train arrives at St Anton in June 1992 behind OBB 1042 612-0. The livery with the white band instead of overall red, adds to the neat design of these engines.

On a beautiful sunny morning in June 2002, 1044 276-2 surmounts the summit at Brenner with EC81 from Munchen to Milano. Of particular note are the class 1012s stabled in the siding, which have since been purchased by Hector Rail in Sweden.

The classic view at St Jodok shows OBB 1822 004-6 rounding the curve with a morning Lienz to Innsbruck service. This is another class some of which were purchased by a company in a different European country, in this case Poland, although they were not used to any extent there.

The CAT (City Airport Trains) service operates between the city and airport at Wien, with this premium service carrying special colours in green, white and black. Over the years, different classes have been used, commencing, as seen here, with the class 1014. CAT 1014 007-7 is seen passing Mannsworth with a Wien Flughafen to Wien Nord train in June 2005.

The sun does not always shine as here at Enns in June 2005, where 1116 241-8 speeds past on its way from Basel to Wien Westbahnhof with the spray flying. This station has now been by-passed by the high speed line from Linz to Wien, so that major expresses are no longer seen at this station. However, it still hosts plenty of freight and local passenger services.

Don't get your wires crossed!! 1116 208-8 and 1061 021-6 stand on the turntable at Villach West shed in June 2005, with the tangle of wires adding to the scene.

The Austrian railways have been one of the major players in giving locomotives colour schemes to recognise various events. In this case, the Austrian Red Cross was recognised on 1116 264-1, which is seen at a celebration in Innsbruck Hbf in May 2006.

A train from Ceske Budejovice to Linz has arrived at Summerau, on the border of the Czech Republic. The CD class 340 has been removed and 1044 085-9 is now ready to depart. The conductor urges me to get on with taking my photo, so that I can get back on the train without delaying it. May 2008.

In 2008, Austria and Switzerland hosted the European Football Cup Final matches, and OBB in particular pioneered decorating locomotives in the colours of the participating countries. The Swiss engine, 1116 075-1 passes Marchtrenk with an eastbound train of autoracks in May that year.

Closely following the previous train at Marchtrenk was a Salzburg to Wien Westbahnhof train headed by 1116 250-0, carrying a colour scheme to celebrate the 250th anniversary of the birth of Mozart in 2006.

Once again the conductor allows me to alight to take a photo as our train waits for the single line section ahead to clear. 4010 016-6 is seen at Klaus working a Graz to Linz train.

In another special livery is 1116 245-8, which celebrates fifty years of the Federal Army. It has stopped at Leoben in May 2008, on its way from Praha to Ljubljana

A few class OBB 1116s have carried logos for Gysev, the jointly owned Austro-Hungarian company which operates trains in both of these nations. But heading somewhat away from its normal sphere of operations, 1116 061-1 passes Villach West with a mixed freight train, passing a car-carrying train stabled at the small station.

With the mountains in the background at Villach West, Hercules diesel 2016 054-5 takes things easy as it nears its destination with a Katschach to Villach Hbf train.

The full glory of a football coloured engine is seen on Netherlands liveried 1116 041-3, which has stopped at Spittal Millstattersee with a Munchen to Zagreb train in May 2008.

At Assling, on the outskirts of Munchen, 1016 023-2 in Kyoto Express colours heads away from the city on its way to Milano in June 2011. Austrian trains are common on this line between Munchen and Rosenheim/Salzburg/Kufstein.

In Front Runner colours, 1116 130-4 comes down from the Semmering Pass and runs through Payerbach-Reichenau with an eastbound Innofreight service in July 2014.

One Railjet set has been decorated in the Austrian national colours. It is seen here at Payerbach-Reichenau, working from Graz to Wien Meidling. 1116 249-4 brings up the rear.

There is a growing number of private operators in Austria, and in this example, *Adria* 1216 920, is seen passing Lanzendorf-Rannersdorf with a northbound intermodal service. The 217 bus to Schwechat waits patiently.

In the attractive surroundings of Tullnerbach-Pressbaum, another private operator, Steiermarkbahn, works an eastbound mixed freight train behind E189 822 in July 2014.

Bulgaria

Class 46/2 is a Koncar rebuild of the Electroputere class 46. Engine 46 243.2 stands at Podujane depot in Sofia in October 2007. (Murray Lewis)

An ADL tour train is seen at Cherkovista near the Romanian border. The three coach train is headed by 07 001.1, of the DB class 232 design. October 2007. (Murray Lewis)

BDZ 07 124.1 is seen with a two-coach passenger train near Dimitrovgrad in September 2011. (Brian Denton)

Of the same design as the Czech class 242 electric locos, 44 179.2, in very clean condition, stands with a freight train at Septemuri. (Brian Denton)

The evening sun casts long shadows at Plovdiv, where 46 125 arrives with a multi-coloured passenger train. (Brian Denton)

Siemens Desiro DMU 30001.6 looks smart in the Bulgarian colours, and is seen at Septemuri with a train bound for Sofia in September 2011. (Brian Denton)

Croatia

In June 1991, 441 726 stops at Karlovac, with a passenger train possibly to Rijeka. (DC Collection)

A three coach train, headed by 1061 103, stands at Rijeka with a train bound for Zagreb in April 2010. This class was of Italian design. (Brian Denton)

GM powered diesel 2063 001 waits to leave Rijeka with a Zagreb service. (Brian Denton)

HZ 1141 217 is ready to leave Ogulin on its way from Rijeka to Zagreb. (Brian Denton)

A more colourful class 1141, number 388, is also seen at Ogulin, with a Rijeka to Zagreb passenger service in April 2010. (Brian Denton)

In a rich blue livery, 2043 002 stands with a mixed freight train at Varazdin. These engines were rebuilds of class 2061 and fitted with electric train heating, which would be rather pointless with this working! (Brian Denton)

Czech Republic

The first of one of the classic Skoda built electric locos, 230 001-0, runs through Breclav in June 2001 with a northbound intermodal service. ZSK 350 003-0 waits to take over the 'Vindobona' Wien Sud to Hamburg from an OBB loco.

A Wien Sud to Hamburg express has now reached Germany at Pirna, with CD 371 015-9 running through to Dresden in June 2005.

Typical of the CD railways having locomotives in one-off colour schemes at that time, June 2005, 742 289-2 stands in Klasterec station with a departmental train. This section was still not electrified for a few more years.

A class 749, known to enthusiasts as Grumpies, because of their exhaust note, or Bardotkies for other more prominent reasons(!), is ready to hand over to an electric loco, having reached one end of the non-electrified section. Loco 749 102-0 has stopped at Kadan with a Cheb to Decin train in June 2005, even though the label in the cab window says Chomutov!

From the platforms at Kadan, locomotives on the SD system, that feeds coal from the pits at Tusimice to the massive power stations at Kadan, can be seen. One of these trains is ready to return to the mines behind 184 504-9. This is one of a class of four Bo-Bo-Bo locomotives, by far the most powerful in the Czech Republic.

On a perfect spring day in May 2007, 363 021-7, in the striking Skupina zig-zag colours scheme, approaches Studenka station on its way from Bohumin to Brno.

Amongst several private operates working on the CD system is OKD, one of whose locos, 181 040-7, is seen at Ostrava in May 2007, hauling a train of coal hoppers.

Another uniquely coloured engine is 754 041-2, which is seen standing at Brno waiting to depart for Okrisky in May 2007. Brno loco shed is reputed to have had a large number of tins of paint in various colours, which had to be used up, hence its notable range of schemes on the locos of this class based there.

In another colour scheme for the 'goggle' style diesels, 754 023-0, with another in what might be considered the 'standard' livery for these engines, run light engines out of Brno h.n. Note the cyclist on the left giving chase.

One of the freight electrics of class 130 is seen at Chocen with a westbound mixed freight train. The engine is 130 010-2 in the standard green and white carried by this class in May 2007.

Skoda built electric 163 062-3 is one of the DC versions of this standard design, the 263 being an AC type and the 363 version being a dual voltage DC/AC class. In the normal green and yellow, the Pardubice to Letovice stopping service has called at Zamrsk.

A number of CD engines carry special colour schemes, such as 363 039-9, which has stopped at Havlickuv Brod with a Zdar nad Sazavou to Kutna Hara service in May 2007.

The class 150 leader, 150 001-5, was specially painted in EuroCity/InterCity colours. It is seen stopped at Olomouc with a Warszawa to Praha international express.

In a totally different scheme for this class, one of the prides of Plzen depot, 754 057-8, gleams in the sun at Furth im Wald. It is about to be replaced by an Arriva class 223, which will take the Praha to Munchen train on to Schwandorf (where it can be seen in *Rails Across Europe – Northern and Western*). Taken in April 2008.

Viamont, a member of the European Bulls freight alliance, operates in the Czech Republic, as seen at Beroun where 750 059-8 leads a sister loco with coal empties heading east in April 2008.

A Cheb to Praha train stops at Karlovy Vary behind 363 078-7, which carries colours celebrating the Czech Olympic team of 2004.

At platform 3 at Cheb, 242 265-7 draws to a halt whilst working from Stribo to Frantiskovy Lazne.

A grab shot of a most colourful engine, 363 084-5, which is seen at Plzen working a Praha to Cheb express in April 2008. The inscription translates as Help the Children.

Many branch lines are operated by railbuses such as the class 810. 810 032-3, which is ready to leave Harazdovice on its journey to Klasterec.

The class 340, of which there are only three engines, is a 15/25kV dual voltage loco, which normally operates on the line between Ceske Budojovice and Summerau in Austria. In April 2008, 340 062-0 is about to leave with a train to Linz. At Summerau it will hand over to an OBB class 1044 (see the Austrian section of this volume). The colour scheme was unique to this class.

The handsome tilting EMUs work services from Praha to Ostrava and via Brno. Set 682 007-0 approaches Brno past the old signal box, with a Wien Sud to Praha express in June 2009.

In yet another livery for the class 754s, 754 049-5 stands in Brno h.n. about to leave for Zdar nad Sazavou, on a wet morning in June 2009. Brno depot certainly knew how to keep their engines in immaculate condition.

The new corporate CD colours start to take hold. 753 771-5 in CD Cargo blue heads a freight train through Kralupy station in August 2010.

Private operator Unipetrol operates several classes of locomotives, some of which are quite old designs. Class 121 056-6, built in 1960, passes Roudnice nad Labem with a northbound train of tank wagons in August 2010.

Still in the old colours, 363 040-7 stands in Praha h.n. with a service for Jihlava. It is seen in June 2011.

The new corporate blue and white for passenger engines has been applied to CD 151 027-0, entering Pardubice station with a Praha to Zvolen train in June 2011.

The new class 380 has clearance to run through into Austria, as illustrated here as 380 010-9 speeds through Felixdorf towards the end of its journey from Praha to Wiener Neustadt, catching the morning sun in July 2014.

Following the lead of the OBB Railjets, CD has also invested in these train sets. 1216 234-5 heads a Praha to Wiener Neustadt Railjet in CD colours past Silberwald between Breclav and Praha in July 2014.

France (South)

A class CC6500 in green livery, which was used for certain engines fitted for third rail working on the Maurienne line, number 6541 stands in Bordeaux St Jean with a passenger train in September 1984. BB9302 is alongside it. (DC Collection)

BB7292 has arrived at Chambery in August 1989 with the Geneva to Barcelona Talgo service. Diesel CC72008 has now coupled on the front to take the train over the non-electrified section as far as Valence via Grenoble. The contrast between the sizes of the diesel and electric locos with the train set catches the eye.

A pair of BB 67400 diesels, led by 67531 stand in Chambery station awaiting departure.

At La Roche-sur-Foron in the Haute Savoie region, BB25172 has arrived with a train from Annemasse, and will now terminate its three coach train.

The narrow gauge Ligne de Savoie operates from St Gervais-les-Bains to Le Chatelard, where it connects with the Swiss who operate it on to Martigny with an interchange at Vallorcine. SNCF set Z604 is seen leaving Chamonix for Vallorcine in August 1989.

An older class of loco still at work in May 1996 is the pre-Second World War BB300 PO-Midi design. Representing the class BB343 is shunting empty coaching stock at Lyon Perrache in May 1996.

An unidentified northbound service departs from Avignon station, being propelled by BB9609.

Catching the late afternoon sun, multi-voltage BB22304 in the new multi-services colours stops at Avignon with a car carrier/sleeping car service to the Netherlands.

In the classic Gran Confort colours, the leader of the CC6500 class, number 6501, passes through Nimes station with a train of SBB stock bound for Lourdes in May 1996.

A triple-headed eastbound intermodal train passes Montpellier behind CC7108, BB8521 and BB8570, the latter two being dead in transit with pantographs down.

Montpellier station in May 1996, with the sun rather head on, shows CC7145 leaving with a southbound passenger service. The CC7100 class held the world speed record for rail for many years.

Sybic BB 26025 rushes through the deserted station at Tournon, using the normally freight-only lines on the west bank of the River Rhone in May 1996.

One of the big diesels, CC72031, hauls a short northbound freight train through Beaune in September 1998.

During the morning, there was a procession of fast moving southbound freight trains through Beaune, an example of which was hauled by BB8132 in what had become the standard grey and orange colours.

Perched on the super-elevated track in Chalons-sur-Soane station, BB22354 is about to stop with its local train from Macon to Dijon in September 1998.

In En Voyage colours, Sybic BB126163 is ready to leave Dijon with a service to Metz in May 2005.

The class A1A-A1A 68000 was much less common than the BB67000 series, and even more so in Fret green and white, since many had been withdrawn prior to this livery being introduced. However, engine number 468536 was photographed on Chalindrey shed in May 2005 to illustrate this combination.

A problem must have befallen the engine CC172141 of this Basle to Paris Est train, since, before it arrived, CC172180 was summoned from Chalindrey shed, to couple onto the front of the train. Now ready to leave Culmont-Chalindrey the two diesels, both in En Voyage colours, make an imposing sight.

Resplendent in Corail colours, BB109290 hauls empty coaching stock out of Dijon station in May 2005.

Greece

One of the ALCO DL500 'world series' locos, A302, is seen in June 1991, probably at Thessaloniki loco shed. (DC Collection)

An unidentified ex-Romanian DEL4000 ALCO engined locomotive starts away from Thessaloniki with a train bound for Athina, which has probably come from Germany. (DC Collection)

A109 stands in Thessaloniki station, with a train to Western Macedonia. (DC Collection)

Co-Co A457 stops at Larissa with an international service to Athina in June 1991. (DC Collection)

Diesel 9202 is at Diakofto, with train 301 from Kalamata to Athina. (DC Collection)

A Siemens-MAN DMU is seen between Monastiraki and Thission stations on the first Metro line in Athina, with the Acropolis in the background. (DC Collection)

Diesel A6462 waits in Korinthos with a train from Athina to either Kalamata via Tripolis, or Patras. It is waiting in the early morning for another train to arrive from the opposite direction. (DC Collection)

On a sunny afternoon in June 1991, an ex-DB class 221 stands in Athina with what is either the Venezia or Acropolis express. (DC Collection)

The modern face of Greek railways is portrayed by 120 021, standing in the Siemens workshops in Linz (Austria) in June 2005.

Hungary

In standard MAV blue and yellow, but carrying Gysev lettering, V43 326 enters Gyor with an eastbound mixed freight train in June 2001, passing another V43 in the loco shed.

V63 049 approaches Gyor with a Gysev service from Szombathely to Budapest Keleti.

A portrait of the classic Russian built M62, which was used extensively throughout Eastern Europe in the post Second World War era. M62 193 is stabled at Szombathely.

A clean diesel M41 2211 has passengers boarding its train, which is due to leave Szombathely for Szentgotthard in June 2001.

An example of through working is seen at Wien Westbahnhof in September 2008, where 1047 010-2 is leaving with a train destined for Budapest Keleti.

Loco 470 010 (the same loco as seen before, but now renumbered) carries the portraits of a famous Hungarian football team. It is seen passing Ekser with a train from Budapest to Lokoshaza in May 2013.

MAV 432 270 propels its train from Szolnok to Budapest Keleti past the very basic station at Rakoskert.

Diesel shunter 448 404 goes about its duties at Budapest Deli station in the evening sunshine in May 2013.

A pair of AWT (Advanced World Transport) engines, with 753 703-8 leading, passes through Budapest Kelenfold with a trainload of cars.

Built by Softronic in Romania and labelled Rolling Stock (whatever that means), MMV 400 795 is stabled in the yards at Budapest Kelenfold.

In pseudo Santa Fe War Bonnet colours, with the addition of the Hungarian national colours in a stripe, Nohab 459 021, owned by Karpat, is also stabled at Budapest Kelenfold in May 2013.

Gysev 470 501 enters Kelenfold station with a Budapest Keleti to Sopron/Szombathely express. The loco is decorated for the 175th anniversary of Sisi, the Empress Elizabeth of Austria.

MAV Nohab M61 109 stands at Kelenfold with a departmental train of flat wagons.

In a striking colour scheme, Softronic built 'Trans Montana' class Co-Co MMV 600 002-4 runs light into the yards at Budapest Kelenfold.

Rail Cargo Hungaria 1116 047-0, a standard Taurus loco, enters the yards at Kelenfold with a train of hopper wagons.

Bombardier TRAXX design 480 016 stands in Nyiregyhaza station with a Budapest Nyugati to Zahony express in May 2013.

Seen from the train window, hence the reflections, Train Hungary 600 082-0 is stabled outside Debrecen.

At the magnificent Eiffel designed station, Budapest Nyugati, 431 158 prepares to leave with an evening service to Szged in May 2013.

Italy

In June 1975, E646 088 is on the outskirts of Bari, approaching its destination with a service from Pescara.

The superb roof arches of Milano Centrale host an unidentified E646 awaiting departure in June 1975.

'Tortoise' E444 074 is backing out of Milano Centrale, having arrived earlier with a Trans European Express.

Parked in a siding near Anzio, E626 383 keeps company with a train of small ballast wagons in June 1975.

On a murky day at Modena in April 1986, E 428 083 is ready to leave the yards with a mixed freight train. (DC Collection)

With a neat set of semaphore signals showing a clear road ahead, one of the ubiquitous Ale 668 EMUs, number 1117, leaves Mantova with a Verona to Bologna service in June 1995.

A pair of engines stand in Firenze S.M.N. On the left is E424 258, and on the right E646 121, both in their respective class colours.

With a nice Dolomite foothills background, E652 015 brings a Munchen to Verona express into Trento station in June 1995. Building work does not detract from the station gardens on the platform.

An ETR 450 Pendolino set rushes past Parma with a Milano to Roma service. Note the dent in the nose, a common feature of this design, where the nose stood proud of the rest of the front end!

One of the American Whitcomb diesels sent to Italy during the Second World War, D143 3036, shunts empty stock at Roma Termini in February 1997, around forty years since it arrived in the country.

Now that is what I call a signal box! The superb structure dominates the scene at Bologna, where E444 106, in the new FS corporate colours, is arriving with a lengthy Milano to Bari express in March 1998.

At Verona Porta Nuova, E402 019, still in its original class colour scheme, starts away with an express from Venezia to Livorno in April 2002.

A close up of a Bombardier class 464, the largest and very successful class in Italy, shows E464 061 waiting at Vicenza with a train bound for Treviso.

Private operator Rail Traction Company operates services in the northern part of Italy. At Brescia, two ex-CD locos, D753 733 and 732 are stabled in May 2005.

Another private operator, NF Cargo, has also acquired ex-CD locos. DE 520-10 FM, with two class E630s in tow, passes Gallarate with a southbound freight train.

RTC EU43 003RT passes Peschiera del Garda in May 2005, with an eastbound freight train. This class regularly works trains from Verona up to Brennero.

Tilo is an organisation that runs trains between Milano and Como. Leaving Milano Centrale, E464 196 pushes its empty stock towards the stabling sidings.

Also in May 2005, FS E412 020 passes Villach West with a freight train. Knowing the penchant of Italians for daubing graffiti on trains, this loco really shows how nice engines can look in these colours, when unadorned.

FS has taken over a number of the 'Astride' locomotives from SNCF, and one such is seen working a southbound freight through Zoagli. Numbered into an Italian series, E436 338 also carries SNCF labels and is seen in May 2014.

In its distinctive livery, Oceanogate E483 020 heads a northbound intermodal service from La Spezia to Melzo through Arquata Scrivia.

GTS operates intermodal services, as in this case working through to the docks at La Spezia. At Solignano, exiting one of the many tunnels through the Apennine Mountains, E483 006 looks as if it could do with a good clean.

In the new Frecciabianca scheme, E402B 104, with its matching coaching set, has stopped at Reggio Emilia whilst working a Milano to Lecce express in May 2014.

The branch from Reggio Emilia to Sassuolo has extensive sidings at Dinazzo where tiles are manufactured. A Dinazzano Po intermodal service heads for Dinazzo behind Vossloh G2000 23, passing Scandia.

Regional operator FER operates many services in the Emilia Romagna region of Italy. With not too much graffiti spoiling the engine, FER E464 391 stands proud in the Italian national colours in the station at Poggio Rusco, waiting to leave for Sermide in May 2014.

Portugal

Bombardier built class 1960, number 1971 stands in Coimbra B station in May 1990 with a train of vans. (DC Collection)

A busy scene at Entroncamento in May 1998, with Eurosprinters 5623 and 5624 stabled in the bay platform next to a single car DMU, whilst 5607 has stopped with a Lisbon SA to Covilha express, and 2611 is on the right with a Lisbon SA to Tomar semi-fast train.

Class 5600 Eurosprinter 5621-6 passes between Coimbra B station platform and the palm tree with a northbound train of cement bags.

The works foreman at Barreiro very kindly brought this engine out into the open for photos to be taken by four British enthusiasts in May 1998. The locomotive is the first of the class 1800s number 1801 which had been restored to its original condition. This class was similar in many respects to the British class 50.

Barreiro station (at which the ferries from Lisbon terminated) hosts CP 1804 with a train due for Vila Real and Lagos in the Algarve region, whilst further back 1525, an Alco design, waits to leave for Evora and Beja.

The Portuguese railways bought locomotives from various sources including Alco, such as 1501, an American RSD5 design, also beautifully restored to its original condition. It is seen stabled at Ermidas Sado in May 1998. One has to wonder what the man on the station roof is doing!

At the neat little station at Tunes, 1209 leaves after its stop with a train from Faro to Lagos. These locos were similar to the SNCF BB63000s.

Patently of French design and similar to the French CC72000s, big diesel 1903 leaves Tunes with a freight train to Faro/Vila Real in May 1998. Note that the engine has a buckeye coupling, not conventional buffers.

A train from Cascais approaches Lisbon Cais do Sodre station in May 1998. This line is unconnected to the rest of the CP network.

Lisbon Oriente station, with its amazing architecture, was constructed in conjunction with the Expo 98 world fair. A Porto to Lisbon SA express has stopped, with Eurosprinter 5611-7 at the head. Many of this class now carry advertising liveries as this example shows. The photo was taken in July 2011.

CP 1429 ambles along past the apartment blocks at Lisbon Oriente with a short container train. Note the design of the OHE masts at the ends of the platforms.

DMU 2253 is about to come to a stop at Vila Franca de Xira with a regional stopping service to Lisbon. Several old buildings, including the station and such as that on the left, make this an interesting location for the tourist.

Also at Vila Franca de Xira, one of the double deck EMUs serving the Lisbon metropolitan area arrives with a local train in June 2011, but who the gentleman leering at the front is, I have no idea. This was the only set seen which was not in just plain green colours.

As with many other countries, multiple units start to replace locomotive hauled trains, as illustrated by a CP class 4000 Pendolino set, working a Porto to Faro train through Santarem.

Some private operators now intrude into Portugal from Spain, such as Takcargo, whose 6005 is heading south through Coimbra B with an intermodal service to Entroncamento. The Co-Co 6000 class diesels are a Vossloh 4000 design.

The latest design of freight loco on CP is the class 4700, one of which, 4711, is seen passing Aveiro in June 2011 with a northbound cement train. This class is built by Siemens as a new universal design based on the Taurus.

Romania

A sparkling Craiova Co-Co electric 40 0405-7 is seen at Craiova depot in June 1994. (DC Collection)

Buceresti Nord station has three trains in the station, the nearest being hauled by Sulzer diesel 60 0804-9 with, further back, two class 40/41 Co-Co electrics, all on regional services to the North and West of Buceresti. (DC Collection)

060EA 1054 has just arrived at Buceresti Nord station with a long distance domestic service. The 060 classification would become class 41. Photographed in June 1994. (DC Collection)

In May 2013, CFR 477 785-6 passes Rakos on the outskirts of Budapest with a late running overnight service from Buceresti to Budapest Keleti.

DBSR 478 001-7 catches me unawares as it speeds through Budapest Kelenfold with an intermodal service heading into the city.

CFR 40 091-3 runs into Kelenfold yard in May 2013, with a lengthy train of box wagons.

Serbia

One of the GM engined diesels used widely through Yugoslavia, and then allocated to the different countries when devolution took place, number 661 112 is seen standing in a siding with a lengthy mixed freight train in June 1990. The location has not been identified. (DC Collection)

ZS 461 001 stands outside Beograd main station in October 2007. This class of Co-Co electrics was built by Electroputere in Romania. (Murray Lewis)

ASEA built 444 002 stands in Beograd main station with a three-coach passenger train. (Murray Lewis)

The remaining loco of four built, which were used amongst other things on the presidential train, Co-Co diesel 666 003 is seen in October 2007 in Beograd Makish yard with a freight train. (Murray Lewis)

Slovakia

ZSSK 721 017-2 stands in Strba station with a ballast train in December 1994. On the right is the rack railway, and the Tatra Mountains are seen in the background. (DC Collection)

Presov allocated 751 033-2 stands in that station with a passenger train for an unknown destination. (DC Collection)

Standing in Bratislava Hlavna Stanica (to give it its full name), 363 135-5 passes the day with a train not ready to run anywhere yet. June 2001.

A Bratislava H.S. to Zvolen train waits to leave behind a very smart 240 132-1. The graffiti crowd have not yet done their worst!

Standing in the yard at Marchegg on the Austrian border, a rather shabby ZSSK 770 073-5, a Skoda product, heads a mixed freight, which will head into Slovakia. The date is June 2001.

Wien Sud as it was in June 2005 sees 754 085-9 accelerate with a puff of exhaust smoke, with a service to Nitra.

The class 350 have been the pride of the fleet for many years, operating major services within Slovakia, as well as running through to Praha. At Trencin in June 2009, 350 014-7, in the unique colour scheme adopted for this class, has stopped with an express from Wien Westbahnhof to Kosice.

A gathering outside the loco shed at Zilina with 163 058-1 in the new ZSSK red and white, accompanied by another class 163, a class 796 shunter and a class 140.

A train destined for Banska Bystrica stands in Zilina station, with 754 082-6 ready and waiting for the departure time in June 2009.

In the new standard colours, 363 134-8 arrives at Puchov with a Kosice to Bratislava express.

A Zilina to Trencin local service has stopped at Puchov in June 2009, headed by 362 002-8, advertising Poistovna. The graffiti hooligans have been at work on the coaches, but not the loco.

A general view at Bratislava HS with 350 015-4 on the right leaving with an express from Praha to Budapest, 240 072-9 stabled in the centre, and on the left 350 011-3 in the new livery.

Only 10 of class 263, a pure AC version, were built, of which ZSSK has eight and CD two. Working into Bratislava HS in June 2009, 263 008-5 leads an empty stock train.

Private operator PSZ loco 240 125-9 heads a lengthy train of GATX leased tanks into Budapest Kelenfold in May 2013.

Slovenia

An unidentified GM engined loco brings a train of hopper wagons out of Bohinj Tunnel at Podbrdo in June 1990. (DC Collection)

Locomotive 664 116 stands in Nova Gorica with a freight train in June 1990. (DC Collection)

The length of the hood of the 664 class is overwhelming when compared to the cab end. This is well illustrated by 664 120-2, which is waiting to leave Jesenice with a southbound freight in June 2005.

The shunter on the front of 642 177 looks suitably bored, as his train returns to the yards at Jesenice, having worked round into an industrial area.

The French built 363 class, similar to the SNCF CC6500, works both passenger and freight services in Slovenia. With a southbound freight ready to leave Jesenice, 363 026 still wears the old brown livery in June 2005.

Engines are changed at Spielfeld-Strass, where SZ takes over from OBB. The OBB Taurus having brought the train from Wien Sud has now left the train and will take charge of a return trip later on. SZ 342 038 has now coupled on to take the Zagreb-bound train through Slovakia in May 2006.

The very smart looking Pendolino 310 004 stands in Maribor station, and will shortly leave for Ljubljana.

One of the typical Italian split-bodied Bo-Bo-Bo designs, 362 032, passes through the yards at Maribor with a southbound freight train.

In the newer colour scheme, which suits it admirably, 363 027 stops at Maribor in May 2006 with a Wien Sud to Rijeka service comprised of a variety of coaching stock. The station clock says 11.55, so it is spot on time.

A pair of what were then new Taurus locos for SZ, 541 005 and 004, pass Marchtrenk in Austria with a westbound freight in May 2006.

Posed at Ljubljana, 644 021 spends a day static in June 2010.

Is there anywhere one can escape the Golden Arches? Based on the DB class 642, Siemens Desiro 312 001 gives full exposure to McDonald's in Ljubljana station.

Several of the Taurus class 541s carry advertising liveries, as exemplified by 541 001, which portrays the international Alpine Convention. It is heading an eastbound intermodal freight past Ljubljana station.

International services pass through Ljubljana each day, illustrated by 541 022, which is entering the station with a train from Beograd to Munchen in July 2010.

Spain

English Electric built 277 202-8, with a class 321 behind, leads a freight train past Leon in September 1984. (DC Collection)

In the old colours, 250 082-0 runs through Tarragona station alongside the shore of the Mediterranean in September 1984. (DC Collection)

'Thunderbird' 276 031-2 enhances Puerta De Atocha station in Madrid, as it stands waiting for something to rescue. This loco is of the same design as the SNCF 7100, but of course with bogies of a different gauge. April 1997

Also present in Madrid for Thunderbird duties was 319 245-7, carrying an AVE colour scheme.

Krauss Maffei Talgo loco 352 005-3, *Virgen del Carmen,* waits for the signal to leave Madrid Chamartin with a train to Hendaye/Bilbao in April 1997. The contrast in size with the class 252 Eurosprinter shows how small the Talgo sets are.

A rather graffitied diesel shunter, 311 125-9, heads a train of loaded car carriers past Fuencarral.

Express DMU 448 001-8 starts away from Guadalajara with a Zaragoza to Madrid service in April 1997. The zig-zagging of the overhead catenary wires is quite clear in this picture. Class 450 double deck Cercanias stock is stabled in the sidings.

The largest class of electric locos in April 1997 was the 269. In the standard grey and yellow at that time, 269 281-2 stands at Aranjuez with a train predominantly of autoracks full of Ford Kas.

A Cercanias train from Guadalajara to Tres Cantos starts away from Vallecas in April 1997, being worked by double deck 450 042M.

A well-loaded northbound ballast train, double headed by 251 016 with 269 037 dead in transit, passes Vallecas.

At Santa Eugenia, 250 011-4 passes with a southbound intermodal, as an EMU appears under the bridge. The four track section from here to Vallecas acts as a by-pass for freight trains around the Eastern side of Madrid, avoiding the city centre. April 1997.

Seen from a train at Albergaria Dos Doze in Portugal in May 1998, an ex-RENFE ALCO DL500 'world series' engine is now in the hands of contractors. It was previously class 416 1603, but whilst it still carries that number in abbreviated form, the old livery has been totally replaced.

A train of what looks like logs is seen in May 1998 near Tudela, headed by class 319 number 219 in an old livery. (DC Collection)

In a barren part of the country, 333 047-9 heads a tank train near Zeneta in August 2000. (DC Collection)

In September 2007, some sectorisation has taken place. In a new colour scheme, Eurosprinter 252 060-9 runs along the line near Ciempozoulos with an express from Valencia to Madrid.

Also near Ciempozoulos, 269 410-7, which has lost its old grey and yellow colours, heads south with a Madrid to Granada Talgo service.

A new corporate colour scheme enhances diesel loco 334 012-2, which is passing the abandoned station at Huerta de Valdacarabanos, working a train from Madrid to Cartagena.

Heading north at Huerta, 333 343-2 wears the Mercanias freight livery as it leads a mixed freight train in the late afternoon in September 2007.

Spanish railways host a number of private operators, an example of which is Continental Rail, whose 333 380-4 is seen passing Villasequilla with a southbound intermodal service.

The high speed line south from Madrid, as seen in September 2007, saw not only class 100 TGV style multiple units, but also some loco hauled trains. Near Esquivias one evening 252 008-3, in AVE colours, dashes past on its way from Barcelona to Cadiz, and didn't we do well to catch the loco number!

Next morning sees set 100 04 at the same location, but heading towards Madrid with a high speed service from Seville.

The Altaria brand is carried by 252 031-0, which rounds the sharp curve into Aranjuez station, with a Gijon to Alicante Talgo train in September 2007. What elegant station lamp posts!

Switzerland

Re 4/4 II 11103 stands in Luzern station with its matched train set, destined for Zurich Flughafen in July 1988.

Running alongside Lake Brienz with a settlement of typical Swiss chalets, an SBB Brunig line train is headed by a class Deh 4/6 loco on its way from Interlaken Ost to Meiringen.

On a dull afternoon in July 1988 not enhanced by a dull coloured locomotive, BLS Ae 6/8 207 stands in the middle road at Interlaken Ost with a freight train.

One of the prototype locos developed for SBB as the next generation of electric locos, Re 4/4 IV 10103 *Luino,* in Bahn 2000 publicity colours, stands with empty stock at Brig in July 1988. This class was later transferred to the SOB line, where it became class 446.

Kleine Scheidegg in July 1988 shows three sets of Jungfraubahn Bdhe 2/4 Emus in the station, with Wengeralpbahn Bdhe 4/4 stock in the distance.

SBB is not known for scrapping rolling stock just because it is old. To illustrate this, 1930s built Ae 4/7 11012, a loco with Buchli drive, stands at Martigny with some coaches in August 1989 – so only at least 50 years old!

Bellinzona shed had an allocation of Re 4/4 Is in the 1980s for operating local services. At Cadenazzo, 10018 is working from Locarno to Bellinzona.

One of the 'Grey Mouse' EuroCity EMUs of class RABe departs from Lugano, working from Zurich to Milano. These were formerly built as Trans European Express trains, hence the TEE logo on the rear. August 1989.

Bodensee Toggenburg Re 4/4 IV 93 *St Gallen* stands on the Zurich line platform at Arth Goldau after arrival in September 1992. The BT merged with the former SOB to form one new SOB line from Romanshorn to Luzern, this loco then being reclassified as a class 456.

A picturesque scene at Rigi Staffel in September 1992, where Rigi Bahn Bhe 4/4 number 31 from Vitznau to the summit at Rigi Kulm has stopped. The line to Arth Goldau descends steeply on the left. The cows are disinterested – they have seen it all before!

Switzerland led Germany and Austria in using locomotives for advertising purposes, the SBB class 460s being decorated in many different schemes. At Intschi in June 1998, 460 022-7, in Swiss Touring Club colours with 460 052-4 in standard SBB red, head north with a freight train.

I was travelling in a Postbus from Erstfeld to Wassen, when we were stopped by temporary traffic lights. Looking through the window, I thought 'wouldn't it be nice if a train came along whilst we were waiting'. Lo and behold, 460 074-8 and 460 073-0 appeared with a northbound freight train, the lead loco in Swiss cargo green. Note that the catenary mast is exactly between the two locos. Good timing? Of course not, photographer's skill!

The classic view at Wassen with the classic loco combination on the Gotthard route in those days – June 1998. Re10/10 combination of 11358 and 11608 head south with an intermodal, the famous church overseeing the train.

One of the original SBB Bahn 2000 class Re 4/4 IVs is seen in the ownership of SudOstbahn near Pfaffikon in July 2001. Now class 446 447-5 carries Tesa colours as it works from Luzern to Romanshorn in beautiful evening sunlight.

Also seen at Pfaffikon was one of the Zurich S-bahn sets of a class 450 with three double deck coaches. 450 096 carries an inscription advertising universal tickets for use on buses, ships, trams and trains in the Zurich area.

An unusual version of advertising colours was seen on Re 6/6 11689, which is moving off Erstfeld shed in order to bank a freight train up to Goschenen. The engine was celebrating the hundreth anniversary of the Swiss loco engineers' trade union, and was seen in July 2001.

The SOB acquired several ex-DR class 109/142 locos, two of which make a colourful combination whilst shunting at Biberbrugg. In front is 477 913-8 Holz, whilst behind is 476 468-4 Classic Rail in July 2001.

Marklin have had many different liveries applied to Swiss (and German) locomotives over the years, but perhaps the most stylish was this design, seen on 460 033-4. The engine was photographed at Morges in June 2002, whilst working an express from Milano to Geneva Airport.

The narrow gauge Rhatische Bahn has operated powerful electric locomotives of various ages and wheel arrangements. The most modern are the Ge 4/4 III type, of which an example is 642 Albula, which is seen at Bever in May 2003, hauling a train from St. Moritz to Chur. The engine celebrates the centenary of the opening of the line through the Albula tunnel, the squiggly line representing the layout of the line between Bergun and Preda. This photo is an example of the extensive narrow gauge main lines in addition to the RhB, such as the MGB, MOB and Brunig lines.

The old Lotschberg BLS route down to Brig descends the side of the River Rhone gorge. Hohtenn station is situated near the top, where four BLS Re 4/4s are climbing up towards the tunnel at Goppenstein with a northbound intermodal train in May 2005. The engine numbers are 163, 165, 186 and 177.

A BLS Nina EMU in a very non-standard colour scheme is about to leave Thun station with a service to Laupen in May 2005.

A triple hauled northbound intermodal train passes Munsingen, with Crossrail 185 564-2 leased from MRCE in the lead in June 2007.

With the mountains framing the background, the new BLS colours are seen on this pair of TRAXX locos, with 486 006-1 leading a northbound intermodal service through Kandersteg.

The small locos providing services for track workers etc. are often overlooked, so to balance this is a picture of BLS Tractor class Tm 235 092-4 with a train of sleepers passing Ausserberg with Tm 235 206-0 in the background in June 2007. These little engines typify many small diesel and electric small units used for shunting at local goods yards or for maintenance duties on the standard gauge Swiss railways, some with platforms and some with small cranes.

Decorated in advance for the 2008 European Football Cup, 460 015-1 has arrived at Basel with an express from Interlaken Ost. Can you see anyone you know?

In freshly applied Swiss Cargo colours, Ae 6/6 610 519-1 exits Muttenz yards and passes Pratteln with a train of hopper wagons in June 2007.

Turkey (in Europe)

The class E40 000 was derived from the SNCF BB17000. Electric loco E 40 083 stands with a diesel loco being serviced behind, at the front of a passenger train at Istanbul Sirkeci in October 1986. (DC Collection)

Standing in the Istanbul suburbs, one of a class of three locos dating from 1955 Alsthom built BB 4003 waits for its next turn of duty. (DC Collection)

Ukraine

Built by Skoda in the late 1960s, ChS4 973 heads a passenger train near Grechany in May 2008. (Murray Lewis)

2TE116 1276A is seen near Grechany in May 2008 with a passenger service. (Murray Lewis)

DS3 013 is a modern electric locomotive, built as a joint venture between DEVZ of Kharkiv and Siemens. It is standing on shed at Zhmerinka in May 2008. (Murray Lewis)

This striking double loco was built by Skoda in 1996 with works numbers 8988-1 and 8988-2. Carrying number ChS7 300, it is seen at Sevastopol in the Crimea in May 2008. (Murray Lewis)

ChS2 467, built by Skoda around 1960, but since rebuilt with new cabs, stands at Simferopol. (Murray Lewis)

In yet another colour scheme, ChS7 299 stands in Dnipropetrovsk station with a daytime express to Kyiv. (Murray Lewis)

Although seen in Kiev passenger depot, ChS4T 433 is not a Ukranian loco, coming from either Russia or Belarus. It is a rebuild of Skoda built ChS4. May 2008. (Murray Lewis)

This modern streamlined design diesel loco is one of four built by Lugansk in 2008. Standing with a mixture of other classes, TEP150 003 is at Kharkiv October depot in May 2010. (Murray Lewis)

A class VL82M multi-voltage double electric loco number 025 heads a freight train through Kupyansk in May 2010. These locos were built at Novocherkassk in Russia in the 1970s. (Murray Lewis)

One of the 3,000 volt DC electrics, VL8M 471, stops in the May sunshine at Krasny Liman. (Murray Lewis)

Having seen every colour scheme under the sun (and outdoing the Czechs in the process!), VL8 853 passes the imposing station building at Krasnoarmeysk with a freight train in May 2010. (Murray Lewis)